Rainy

By Alice K. Flanagan

Drip, drip. Splash!
Here comes the rain!

Rain bounces off the ground.

Rain falls down hard in a park.

There are many kinds of rainfall. A **sprinkle** is light. A **downpour** is heavy.

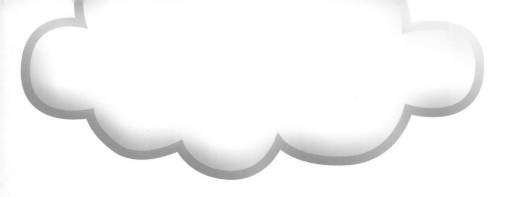

Rain is part of the **water cycle**. How does water become rain? First, the sun heats water in lakes, rivers, and oceans.

The sun heats the water in a lake.

Gas rises off the water's surface.

As water heats up, it turns into **gas**. You cannot see the gas as it rises into the cooler air in the sky. Then the gas cools, too.

The gas turns into tiny drops of water. The drops form clouds. The drops become too heavy to stay in the air. Then they fall as rain.

Rain clouds gather in the sky.

The water cycle looks like this.

Rain falls onto the soil. Then it flows into rivers, lakes, and oceans. The water cycle begins again.

It takes about 15 minutes for rain to reach the ground. The time depends on how high the clouds are.

Rain falls on the surface of a lake.

Deserts do not get much rain.

In some places, the rain might not even reach the ground. It dries up before it gets there. This happens when the air near the ground is very warm. The warm air turns the rain back into a gas.

Rain can be good. It helps plants grow. It cleans the air of dust and **pollution**. But too much rain can be bad. It can cause a **flood**. A flood can harm people and animals.

Rain has flooded this road.

Playing in the rain can be fun!

The next time it rains, remember that it is all part of the water cycle!

Glossary

downpour (DOWN-por): A downpour is a heavy rain. A downpour brings a lot of water.

flood (FLUD): A flood happens when there is too much water for a certain space. A flood can cause harm.

gas (GAS): A gas is what a liquid turns into when it is heated. The sun turns water into gas.

pollution (puh-LOO-shun): Pollution is something that harms the environment. Rain can help clean pollution out of the air.

sprinkle (SPRING-kul): A sprinkle is a light rain. A sprinkle brings a small amount of water.

water cycle (WAH-tur SY-kul): The water cycle is the constant movement of Earth's water. Rain is part of the water cycle.

To Find Out More

Books

Farndon, John. *Weather: Explore the World of Sun, Snow, and Rain.* New York, NY: DK Publishing, 2017.

Spurr, Elizabeth. *In the Rain.* Atlanta, GA: Peachtree Publishers, 2018.

Thompson, Carol. *Rain.* Bridgemead, Swindon, UK: Child's Play, 2014.

Websites

Visit our website for links about rain:
childsworld.com/links

Note to Parents, Teachers, and Librarians: We routinely verify our Web links to make sure they are safe and active sites. So encourage your readers to check them out!

Index

About the Author

Alice K. Flanagan lives with her husband in Chicago, Illinois, and writes books for children and teachers. Today, she has more than 70 books published on a wide variety of topics, from U.S. presidents to the weather.

The Child's World®
childsworld.com

Published by The Child's World®
1980 Lookout Drive • Mankato, MN 56003-1705
800-599-READ • www.childsworld.com

Photo credits: Arisa_J/Shutterstock.com: 12; Ciolanescu/Shutterstock.com: 15; Daimond Shutter/Shutterstock.com: 16; ehrlif/Shutterstock.com: 8; Evgeny Atamanenko/Shutterstock.com: 3; FamVeld /Shutterstock.com: cover, 1; istanbulphotos/Shutterstock.com: 11; Markus Gebauer/Shutterstock.com: 19; Sunny Forest/Shutterstock.com: 7; Vadym Zaitsev/Shutterstock.com: 4; Yuganov Konstantin/Shutterstock.com: 20

ISBN Hardcover: 9781503827899
ISBN Paperback: 9781622434572
LCCN: 2018939776

Printed in the United States of America • PA02398